Forests
INSIDE OUT

James Bow

CRABTREE
Publishing Company
www.crabtreebooks.com

Author: James Bow
**Publishing plan research
    and series development:** Reagan Miller
Editors: Sarah Eason, Jennifer Sanderson
    and Shirley Duke
Proofreaders: Katie Dicker, Wendy Scavuzzo
Editorial director: Kathy Middleton
Design: Paul Myerscough
Cover design: Paul Myerscough
Photo research: Jennifer Sanderson
**Production coordinator and
    Prepress technician:** Tammy McGarr
Print coordinator: Katherine Berti

Written and designed for Crabtree Publishing
    by Calcium Creative

Photo Credits:

t=Top, bl=Bottom Left, br=Bottom Right

Corbis: Wayne Lynch/All Canada Photos: p. 1, p. 15b; Getty Images: Auscape/UIG: p. 19b; Shutterstock: Lynea p. 9b; Aleksander Bolbot: p. 12–13; Andaman: p. 11b; Cuson: p. 28–29; Dr. Morley Read: p. 8–9; Dugdax: p.28b; Ethan Daniels: p. 20–21; Heiko Kiera: p. 25b; Karen Faljyan: p. 17b; Mark McElroy: p. 6–7; Mayur Kotlikar: p. 27b; Milosz M: p. 4–5, p. 10–11, p. 18–19; Pi-Lens: p. 1, p. 14–14; Pisaphotography: p. 24–25; Sokolov Alexey: p. 13b; TFoxFoto: p. 26–27; Welcomia p. 3, p 16–17; Wikimedia Commons: Will Iredale p. 22–23; Matt Knoth p. 21b, SB Johnny p. 23t.

Cover: Shutterstock: Piotr Krzeslak; Mark Medcalf (br).

Library and Archives Canada Cataloguing in Publication

Bow, James, 1972-, author
    Forests inside out / James Bow.

(Ecosystems inside out)
Includes index.
Issued in print and electronic formats.
ISBN 978-0-7787-1495-8 (bound).--
ISBN 978-0-7787-1500-9 (pbk.).--
ISBN 978-1-4271-7656-1 (pdf).--ISBN 978-1-4271-7652-3 (html)

    1. Forest ecology--Juvenile literature. 2. Forest animals--
Juvenile literature. 3. Forests and forestry--Juvenile literature.
I. Title.

QH541.5.F6B683 2015   j577.3   C2014-907847-1
                                              C2014-907848-X

Library of Congress Cataloging-in-Publication Data

Bow, James, author.
 Forests inside out / James Bow.
    pages cm. -- (Ecosystems inside out)
 Includes index.
 ISBN 978-0-7787-1495-8 (reinforced library binding : alk. paper) -- ISBN 978-0-7787-1500-9 (pbk. : alk. paper) -- ISBN 978-1-4271-7656-1 (electronic pdf : alk. paper) -- ISBN 978-1-4271-7652-3 (electronic html : alk. paper)
 1. Forest ecology--Juvenile literature. 2. Forest animals--Juvenile literature. 3. Forests and forestry--Juvenile literature. I. Title. II. Series: Ecosystems inside out.

 QH541.5.F6 B675
 577.3--dc23
                                              2014046707

Crabtree Publishing Company
www.crabtreebooks.com   1-800-387-7650

Printed in Canada/022015/IH20141209

Published in Canada
Crabtree Publishing
616 Welland Ave.
St. Catharines, Ontario
L2M 5V6

Published in the United States
Crabtree Publishing
PMB 59051
350 Fifth Avenue, 59th Floor
New York, New York 10118

Published in the United Kingdom
Crabtree Publishing
Maritime House
Basin Road North, Hove
BN41 1WR

Published in Australia
Crabtree Publishing
3 Charles Street
Coburg North
VIC, 3058

Contents

What Is an Ecosystem?

Plants and animals need many things to survive. They need sunshine, air and water, good soil, and temperatures that are neither too cold, nor too hot. These and other nonliving things that help them live are called **abiotic factors**. Plants and animals also need each other to survive. They are each other's **biotic factors**. An **ecosystem** is made up of **organisms**, the environment in which they live, and their **interrelationships**.

How Big Are Ecosystems?

Ecosystems can be as large as a forest, or as small as a log. A large geographical area that contains similar plants, animals, and environments is called a **biome**. Tundras, oceans, and deserts are biomes.

What Is a Forest Ecosystem?

Forests are areas where trees **dominate** the landscape. Most forests have four parts: the floor, the understory, canopy, and the **overgrowth** or emergent layer. There are other plants in the ecosystem, but trees have the greatest effect. As a result, the other organisms in the ecosystem build their lives around trees.

Let's explore the ecosystems found in the forests of the world. As we go through this book, we will look at each ecosystem as a whole, then zoom in on one part of it.

What Is a System?

A system is a group of separate parts that work together for a purpose. The living parts of an ecosystem depend on the nonliving factors in the ecosystem to stay healthy, live, and reproduce. Every part of the system has an important role to play. A healthy ecosystem has many different plants and animals living together. If any part of the ecosystem changes or fails, the other parts can be affected.

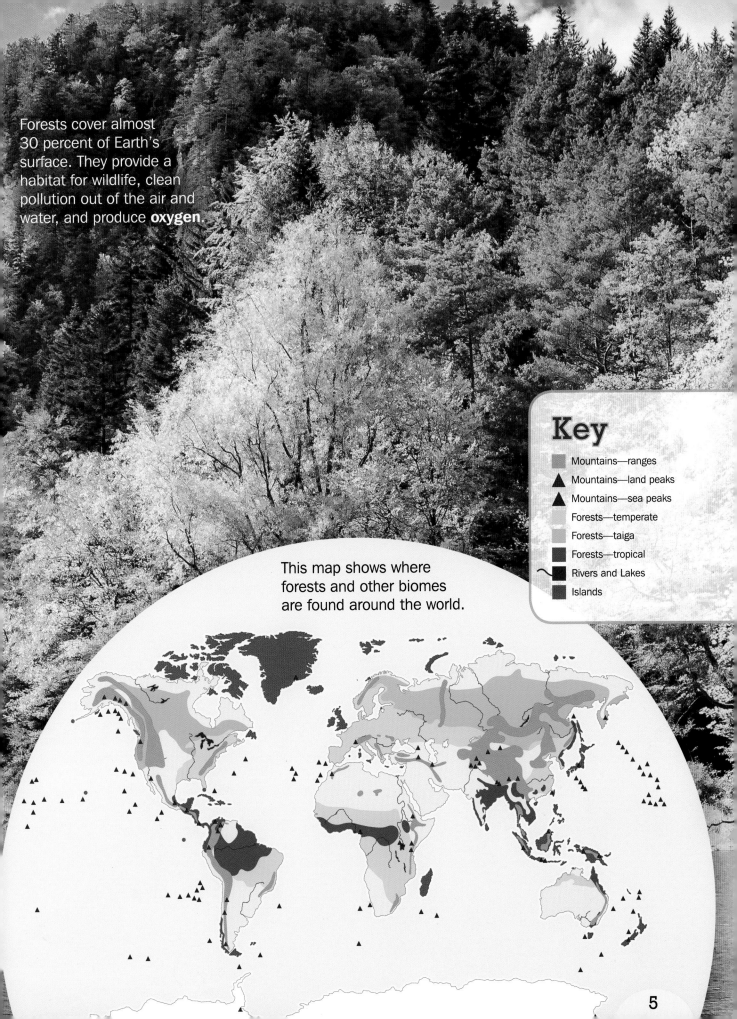

Forests cover almost 30 percent of Earth's surface. They provide a habitat for wildlife, clean pollution out of the air and water, and produce **oxygen**.

This map shows where forests and other biomes are found around the world.

Key

- Mountains—ranges
- ▲ Mountains—land peaks
- ▲ Mountains—sea peaks
- Forests—temperate
- Forests—taiga
- Forests—tropical
- Rivers and Lakes
- Islands

Energy in Ecosystems

sun

Organisms cannot live without energy. The sun provides this energy, and organisms spread it through the ecosystem as food. This is known as a **food web** or a **food chain**. Within this web, organisms fall into one of three groups: producer, consumer, or decomposer.

Chain of Energy

Producers make their own food from sunlight through a process called **photosynthesis**. In this process, organisms use **chlorophyll** to convert water from soil and **carbon dioxide** from air to produce sugar and oxygen. Producers include plants and **algae**. In forests, trees are the main producers.

Animals cannot get their energy from sunlight. They must eat producers or organisms that eat producers. Herbivores are animals that eat plants, while carnivores eat herbivores and other carnivores. Omnivores eat plants and animals.

Decomposers are organisms, such as **bacteria** and **fungi**, that break down dead plant and animal matter. They put **nutrients** back into the soil. Plants use the nutrients to grow and the food chain begins again.

Diverse Ecosystems

In a forest, there are many **species** playing the roles of producers, consumers, and decomposers. This is called **biodiversity**.

tree

cricket

mouse

skunk

This food chain shows the flow of energy from one organism to another.

The energy of the forest comes from the sun. Trees grow tall, competing with each other to grab as much sunlight as they can.

Eco Up Close

A mushroom is a type of fungi that feeds off dead plants and animals. The mushroom grows from a **spore**. The spore produces a fast-growing **fruiting body**, which is the part of the mushroom that releases spores. The spores are carried on the wind to other parts of the forest to grow into more mushrooms. Many mushrooms are good at digesting the cells of dead trees. By doing so, they provide an essential role in the forest ecosystem—mushrooms help trees rot faster and release their nutrients into the soil. Plants and animals use those nutrients to grow.

Tropical Rain Forests

Tropical rain forests are forests found in warm, tropical areas with hot summers and mild winters. They get a lot of rain for most of the year. The trees are **evergreen** because there is no need for them to shed their leaves with the changing seasons. Examples of tropical rain forests include the Amazon Rain Forest, the forests of the Congo Basin in Africa, and the forests of southeast Asia.

A Thick Green Cloud

Tropical rain forests have a thick canopy of leaves that gather energy from the sun and take in moisture from the air. The leaves are so thick, they prevent sunlight and water from reaching the ground. This makes it difficult for smaller plants and trees to grow beneath the canopy. Some plants **adapt** by climbing on the larger trees and growing on their branches.

Animals have also adapted to life in the canopy. The most common **mammal** in the tropical rain forest is the bat. There are more than 50 species of bats in the tropical rain forests of the world, from the tiny bumblebee bat of Thailand to the gigantic flying fox bat with its 6-foot (1.8 m) wingspan. Most food in the rain forest is found up high, so the bat's wings and ability to fly give it an **advantage** over many other animals.

The lush forest provides energy for a large food web. Millions of insects are eaten by birds, such as flycatchers, and **amphibians** such as the poison arrow frog. Herbivores include the slow-moving sloth that hangs from trees and eats shoots, buds, and leaves. **Predators** include jaguars, eagles, and the anaconda.

Eco Focus

Rain forests can create their own rain, and are good at holding onto moisture. When rain forests are cut down, there are no leaves to stop the sun from reaching the ground so the soil dries out. In the hot tropics, what ecosystem might appear if the rain forest disappears? What effect would any kind of change in the nonliving part of an ecosystem have on its food web and biodiversity?

Tropical rain forests cover about 7 percent of Earth's surface.

Eco Up Close

Bromeliads are a family of flowering plants that can be found in tropical areas. There are more than 2,700 species of bromeliads, but the best-known is the pineapple. Many bromeliads have adapted to grow on trees. This helps them get closer to the forest canopy, where they can get more sunlight. The bromeliads' thick, overlapping leaves catch and hold water. The pools of water on the leaves provide tiny ecosystems for small insects and frogs.

bromeliad

Tropical Dry Forests

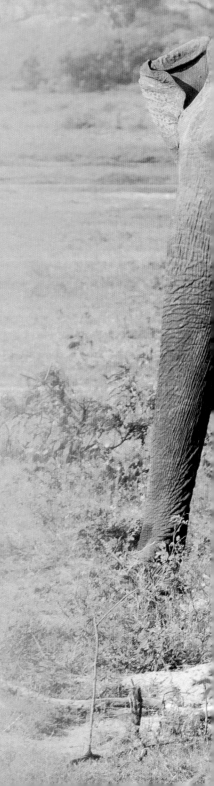

In many places in the tropics, there is very little rain. Some places are wet for part of the year, but have long dry seasons. The forests that grow in these places have adapted to live in those conditions. They are known as tropical dry forests. Examples are the East Deccan forests of southeastern India, the forests of Sri Lanka, and some forests in southern Mexico.

Losing Leaves

In the dry forests, many trees do not hold onto their leaves year-round. Instead, to save energy and water during the dry season, trees such as teak and mountain ebony lose their leaves. These types of trees are called **deciduous**. When deciduous trees lose their leaves, sunlight can reach the forest floor. This allows smaller trees and plants to grab the sun's energy. Dry forests often have a rich understory because small trees and plants grow well in the forests.

Surviving During the Dry Season

The animals that live in dry forests have adapted to live with the changes taking place between the wet and dry seasons. Lemurs are long-tailed mammals that are found in a number of dry forests. They eat insects and lizards, as well as fruit and flowers. During the dry season, there is less food so some lemurs **hibernate**, or sleep. The fat-tailed dwarf lemur of Madagascar can hibernate for seven months, waking only when the rains return. In Africa, the dry forests provide **habitat** and shelter for a number of animals found in nearby grasslands and **savannas**, such as giraffes and lions. The habitats are similar, except the dry forests have more trees.

For dry forests to survive, however, the rains must return. If the dry conditions continue for too long, the trees could die and the forest would be replaced by savanna or desert.

The Sri Lankan dry evergreen forests are home to one of Asia's largest groups of elephants. The ecosystem is protected to help provide a safe place for this endangered species.

Eco Up Close

The Sri Lankan leopard is the **apex predator** of the tropical dry forests of Sri Lanka. These big cats hunt on their own, eating spotted deer, wild boars, and monkeys. The species is **endangered** because people have built on its habitat and hunted many of the animals there.

Sri Lankan leopard

Temperate Broadleaf Forests

Temperate broadleaf forests are found north of the tropics. Many are in eastern North America, western Europe, and parts of Russia, China, and Japan. Summers in these forests are warm and rainy, while winters are cold and snowy. At least 3 to 6 feet (91 to 183 cm) of rain falls there each year.

Spring and Fall

The trees of temperate forests are mostly deciduous. They include oak, maple, and birch. In spring and summer, these trees produce large, flat leaves to catch sunlight. In fall, the trees stop producing chlorophyll in their leaves. The leaves lose their green and change to shades of red, gold, purple, and brown. The leaves make a beautiful show of color. The trees drop their leaves, leaving only bare branches in winter. This helps them save energy. The trees are then **dormant** through winter, before waking and producing new leaves in spring.

The fallen leaves add to the rich soil in temperate forests. Mosses, ferns, and wildflowers grow in the **fertile** soil. Worms and insects eat the leaves and provide food for birds and small mammals. Deer and moose eat the plants, while larger predators such as coyotes and wolves eat other animals. During fall, these animals must find ways to survive through the winter when food is hard to find. Many animals, such as squirrels, build up fat in their bodies during fall to last them through the winter. Others, such as bears, hibernate until spring comes and food returns.

Broadleaf forests drop their leaves every fall, as growing new leaves in the spring takes less energy than trying to keep leaves alive through the cold winter.

Eco Up Close

The black woodpecker is a species found in the temperate forests of western Europe, Siberia, and China. Like other woodpeckers, it eats insects and grubs from dead trees, pecking holes in the wood to pull out the grubs. This helps protect other trees from **burrowing** insects. The black woodpecker does not **migrate**. Instead, it uses a hole it makes in a tree as a **nesting chamber**, sheltering it from the cold. The holes woodpeckers make are also used as homes by other animals such as squirrels.

black woodpecker

Taiga Forests

The most northerly forests are known as taiga, or boreal forests. These are found at latitudes of between 50° and 60° North in northern Canada, Alaska, Siberia, and Scandinavia. In these forests, summers are cool and short, and winters are long and very cold.

A Hard World

The trees in boreal forests are mostly **coniferous**, and include pine, spruce, and fir. These trees have adapted to the cold better than the deciduous trees farther south. Not only must these trees survive the cold winters, when there is little sunlight, but the soil they grow in is shallow and poor, too. The cold weather also slows down decomposers. This means that dead plants and animals are broken down more slowly. As a result, fewer nutrients are returned to the soil.

Taiga forest trees provide food and shelter for more than 85 species of mammals, 130 species of fish, and 32,000 species of insects. During the summer, many birds fly north to these forests. They take advantage of the long days of sunlight during the short summers, and nest and breed before migrating south again in late fall. In summer, herbivores such as moose and caribou eat bark and leaves, as well as plants that bloom, or flower. This helps build up fat reserves that will keep them alive through winter when food is scarce. Wolves, black bears, and grizzly bears are among the apex predators in taiga forests. Some animals, such as bears, survive winter by hibernating. They wake up hungry in spring and eat young tree shoots, and nuts that squirrels buried before the snow fell.

Many coniferous trees have special resins in their sap that act like anti-freeze, stopping sharp ice crystals from forming. The small needles prevent the trees from losing moisture.

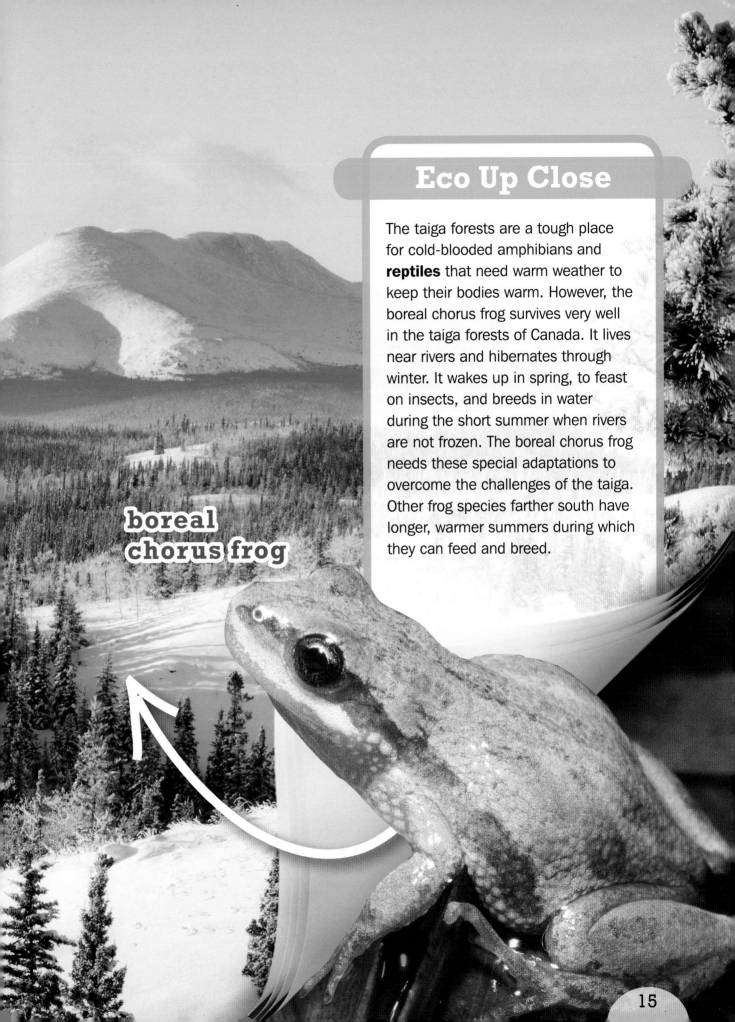

Eco Up Close

The taiga forests are a tough place for cold-blooded amphibians and **reptiles** that need warm weather to keep their bodies warm. However, the boreal chorus frog survives very well in the taiga forests of Canada. It lives near rivers and hibernates through winter. It wakes up in spring, to feast on insects, and breeds in water during the short summer when rivers are not frozen. The boreal chorus frog needs these special adaptations to overcome the challenges of the taiga. Other frog species farther south have longer, warmer summers during which they can feed and breed.

boreal chorus frog

Montane Forests

Montane forests grow on the sides of mountains. In tropical areas, they are called cloud forests. These forests exist because the mountains they grow on force winds at the bottom of the mountain to blow up to its top. As the wind travels upward, its air cools. As the air cools, it drops its moisture as rain. Montane forests usually start at an elevation, or height, of 3,000 feet (914 m) above sea level. Tropical cloud forests, which are found nearer the **equator**, are hotter. The trees there can live higher on the mountain, at heights of 6,562 to 11,483 feet (2,000 to 3,500 m).

Tough Living

Montane forests have to adapt to a number of challenges. The air is thinner high on the mountain, and more of the sun's **ultraviolet** rays reach the ground. The cool temperatures slow down decomposers. As a result, fewer dead animals and plants are broken down, and there are fewer nutrients in the soil. Despite these tough conditions, the trees survive. They provide shelter for a large number of insects and birds, and herbivores such as moose. In turn, these animals are food for larger predators, such as wolves.

Giant sequoia trees can live for up to 3,000 years, grow as tall as a 30-story building, and be wider than a two-lane highway. Their cousins, the giant redwoods, don't live as long but they can grow a lot taller!

Eco Focus

Sequoia trees are found in a very small habitat range on the western slopes of the Sierra Nevada Mountains and the coastal mountains of Oregon, where winds from the west blow in from the Pacific Ocean. What is it about these western slopes that allows sequoia trees to grow there and nowhere else in the world?

Eco Up Close

The largest and tallest trees in the world are found on the western slopes of the Sierra Nevada Mountains in California, the coastal mountain forests of Oregon, and the mountain slopes of the Hubei region of China. The sequoia, or giant redwood, starts life as a seed just 1 inch (2.5 cm) long, but can grow to be 379 feet (115 m) tall! It can also live to be 2,000 years old. The thick bark and the long trunk helps protect the tree from insects and fire. The General Sherman redwood tree in Sequoia National Park in California is the world's largest tree by volume. It is 275 feet (84 m) tall and 103 feet (31 m) around at its base.

sequoia
seed cone

Swamps and Mangrove Forests

Although trees need water to survive, most trees do not like growing in water, because the water drowns the roots by preventing air from entering them. Some trees, however, have adapted to grow in swampy ground, and even in salt water. Swamps and mangrove forests are found in tropical coastlines. There, ocean tides carry saltwater to **estuaries**, **salt marshes**, or **tidal flats**. Mangrove forests can be found in Florida, the Caribbean, and on the coasts of Central America. They are also found in Columbia, Ecuador, Brazil, West Africa, Madagascar, Southeast Asia, Indonesia, and northern Australia.

Shelter and Protection

Mangrove trees are the **keystone species** of mangrove ecosystems. By growing in these wet conditions, they shade the water, which keeps it cool. The trees' roots provide shelter for a number of animals and their young, including oysters, sponges, shrimps, and mud lobsters. The mangroves hold the soil together, protecting it from **erosion** (wearing away) by the ocean waves. The trees also protect other ecosystems farther inland by providing a buffer, or wall, against the ocean. This blocks and absorbs storm surges and tsunamis that would damage drier ecosystems.

Mangrove forests have adapted to grow in water, but they cannot survive freezing temperatures. These mangrove roots have been revealed because the tide is out. When the tide comes in, the roots will be covered with water once more.

Eco Focus

As much as 35 percent of the mangrove forests of the world have disappeared in the past few decades as a result of pollution and development, or building. What could the effect on ecosystems be in these areas where the mangroves have disappeared?

Eco Up Close

The mangrove monitor is a lizard found in the mangrove swamps of northern Australia, New Guinea, and Polynesia. It can grow up to 4 feet (1.2 m) long. Its tail is almost twice the length of its body and the animal uses this long paddle to swim. It eats the eggs of other reptiles and birds, as well as mollusks, insects, crabs, and any carrion, or dead animals, it finds. The monitor lizard was recently introduced to the Marshall Islands in the Pacific Ocean to reduce the rat population there. When the rat population dropped, however, the monitor lizards started eating the chickens of local farmers. Today, the monitor lizards are a bigger problem for farmers than the rats they were brought in to kill.

mangrove monitor

Kelp Forests

Kelp forests are found in the ocean, close to the Pacific coast of North America, Russia, and Japan. There are also kelp forests off the coast of South America, South Africa, Australia, and western Europe. These forests are not full of trees. Kelp is an algae that, over time, has grown leaf-like structures called blades. The blades absorb energy from the sun through photosynthesis. Root-like structures help kelp grip the sea floor, and gas-filled bladders keep the kelp's blades floating near the ocean surface.

Kelp forests need sunlight, so they grow in shallow water where the light can still penetrate. They are rarely found below 131 feet (40 m).

Ocean Life

Kelp may not be a tree, but kelp forests are very much like forests on land. They have a canopy of leaves to catch the sun, a floor, and places in between that allow different plants and animals to survive. Kelp forests are among the most productive ecosystems on the planet. The kelp grows fast using sunlight, oxygen, and nutrients from the ocean, and its blades are eaten by many types of animals, such as sea snails and sea urchins. The kelp also provides shelter for animals such as fish, helping them hide from larger predators.

Eco Focus

Kelp is a fast-growing algae. Like corn, kelp can be taken and put through a process to make sugar, which can be turned into a fuel called ethanol. This fuel does not produce dangerous pollution in the way that fuels such as gasoline do. How could using kelp to make ethanol help in the fight against global **climate change**?

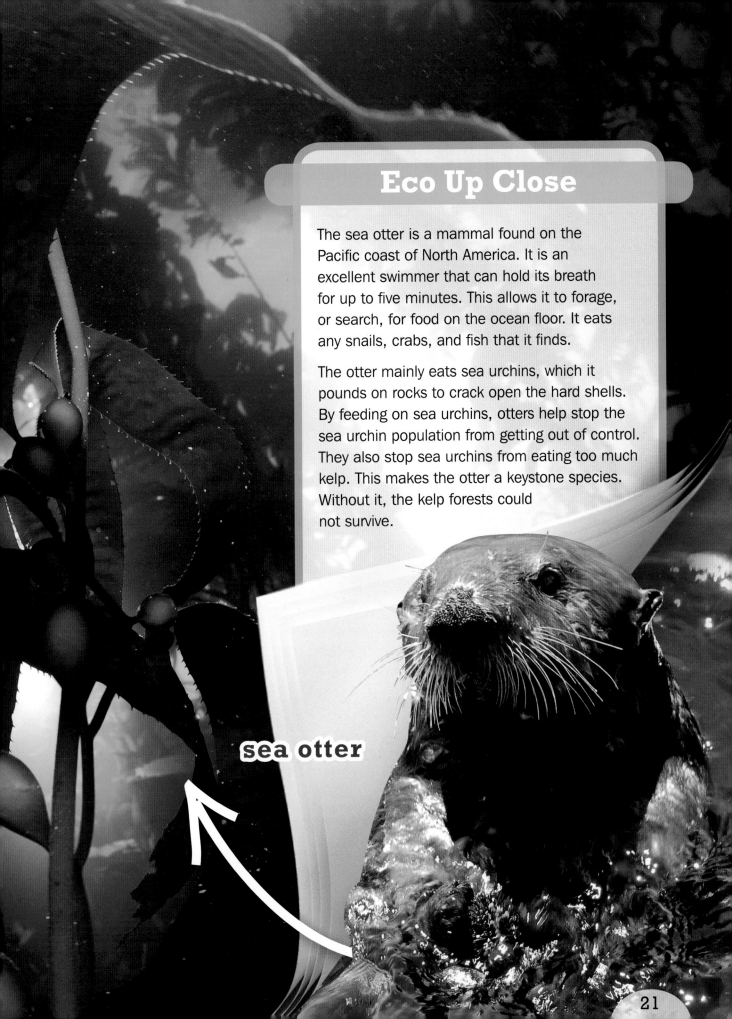

Eco Up Close

The sea otter is a mammal found on the Pacific coast of North America. It is an excellent swimmer that can hold its breath for up to five minutes. This allows it to forage, or search, for food on the ocean floor. It eats any snails, crabs, and fish that it finds.

The otter mainly eats sea urchins, which it pounds on rocks to crack open the hard shells. By feeding on sea urchins, otters help stop the sea urchin population from getting out of control. They also stop sea urchins from eating too much kelp. This makes the otter a keystone species. Without it, the kelp forests could not survive.

sea otter

Plantation Forests

Plantation forests are forests that have been planted by people who cut down the trees for wood or to make paper. Today, there are plantation forests all over the world. They cover more than 652 million acres (264 million ha) and make up more than 7 percent of the world's forests.

Not So Natural

Plantations allow people to harvest, or cut down, many kinds of trees without needing to cut down natural forests. However, plantation forests are usually grown in places where natural forests once grew. Without the biodiversity of a natural forest, plantation forests are not natural ecosystems. The trees are usually young, and often all the same species. The species of tree might not even be **native**, or natural, to the area. There is no mixture of canopy and understory, leaving no chance to build up the fertile soil that is found in natural forests. Plantation forests are not able to provide plants and animals with a habitat that is as healthy as habitats found in natural forests.

Like large farms that grow just a single species of crops, plantation forests are examples of **monoculture**. Without the diversity, or mixture, of species to provide balance within the ecosystem, parts of plantation forests can grow out of control. Plantations are also very vulnerable to disease because all the trees are one species, making it easier to pass the disease on to the next tree. If a disease infects just one tree, it can wipe out an entire forest.

Plantation forests may offer a source of wood that is not from natural forests, but some natural forests have been cleared just so plantation forests can be put in their place.

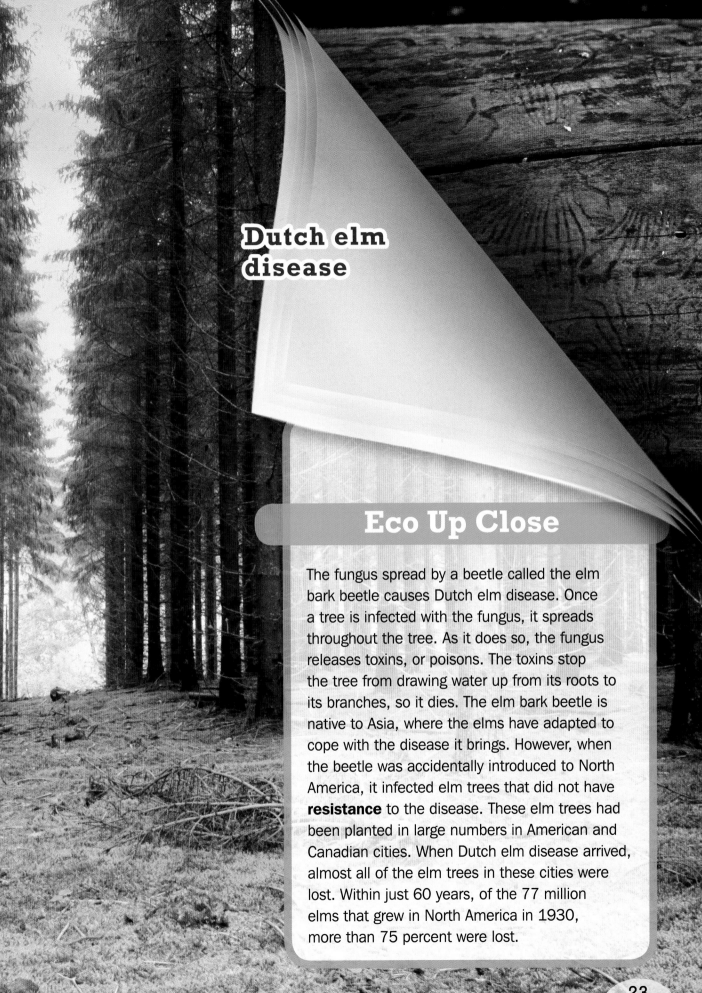

Dutch elm disease

Eco Up Close

The fungus spread by a beetle called the elm bark beetle causes Dutch elm disease. Once a tree is infected with the fungus, it spreads throughout the tree. As it does so, the fungus releases toxins, or poisons. The toxins stop the tree from drawing water up from its roots to its branches, so it dies. The elm bark beetle is native to Asia, where the elms have adapted to cope with the disease it brings. However, when the beetle was accidentally introduced to North America, it infected elm trees that did not have **resistance** to the disease. These elm trees had been planted in large numbers in American and Canadian cities. When Dutch elm disease arrived, almost all of the elm trees in these cities were lost. Within just 60 years, of the 77 million elms that grew in North America in 1930, more than 75 percent were lost.

Urban Forests

Urban forests describe trees that grow in towns and cities. These trees may be survivors of forests that once grew in the places where the cities now stand. They can also be planted by people who live in the cities. Urban forests also include city parks. Central Park is an 843-acre (341-ha) oasis in the middle of New York City. It has more than 25,000 trees, including 1,700 elms. The North Saskatchewan River valley parks system in Edmonton is the largest urban parkland in North America. It stretches 30 miles (48 km) through the city, and there are plans to plant even more trees there.

A Connection to Nature

Cities spend millions of dollars planting and maintaining trees. Despite the cost of looking after urban forests, most city people want to keep them. Trees provide shade on hot summer days, which helps reduce the amount of air conditioning that buildings use. Trees help clean the air by absorbing pollutants through their leaves. They also slow down the flow of rainwater, keeping storms from overwhelming sewer systems. Trees are a habitat for birds and small animals, giving city people an important connection to nature.

As our understanding of the **ecology** of forests has improved, we have become better at managing our urban forests. Cities are now planting more trees that are natural to the local environment, rather than species from different ecosystems. After Dutch elm disease cost many American cities their trees, cities are planting a more diverse range of trees. This will protect our urban forests.

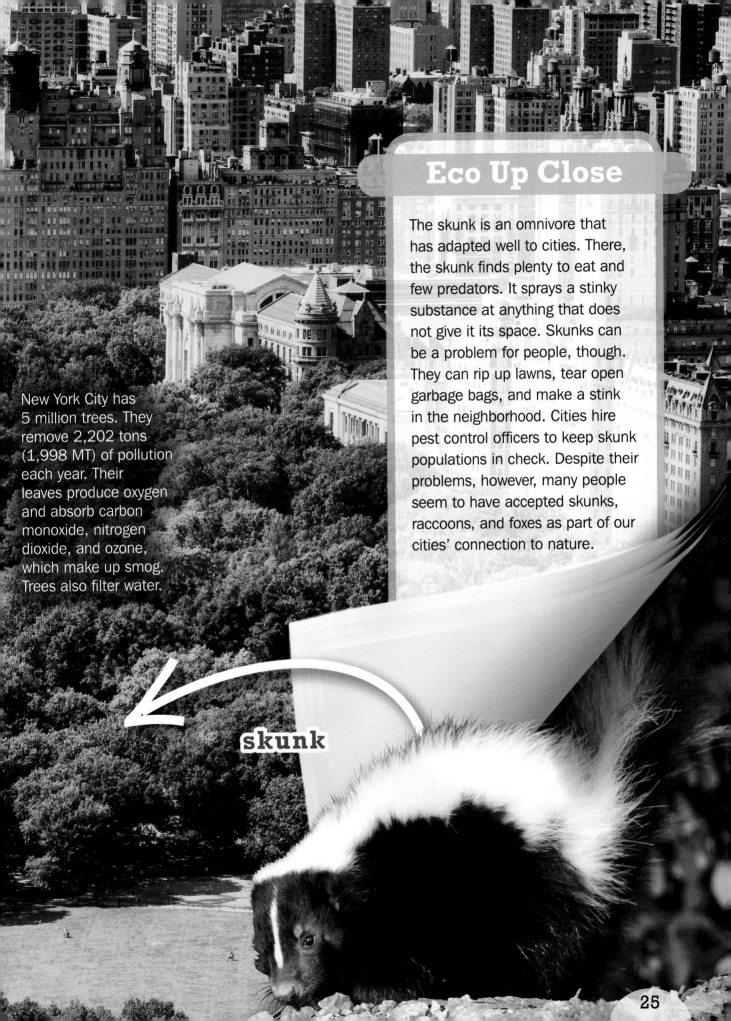

Eco Up Close

The skunk is an omnivore that has adapted well to cities. There, the skunk finds plenty to eat and few predators. It sprays a stinky substance at anything that does not give it its space. Skunks can be a problem for people, though. They can rip up lawns, tear open garbage bags, and make a stink in the neighborhood. Cities hire pest control officers to keep skunk populations in check. Despite their problems, however, many people seem to have accepted skunks, raccoons, and foxes as part of our cities' connection to nature.

New York City has 5 million trees. They remove 2,202 tons (1,998 MT) of pollution each year. Their leaves produce oxygen and absorb carbon monoxide, nitrogen dioxide, and ozone, which make up smog. Trees also filter water.

skunk

People and Forests

The world we live in could not have been built without trees. Without them, we would have no wood, no buildings, and very little furniture to put in the buildings. However, to get that wood, we are cutting down our forests faster than they can grow back. This is called deforestation. Since the 1850s, half of the world's tropical forests have been cut down to make space for farmland or to build cities. In 2005, the United Nations estimated that Earth's total forest area is decreasing at a rate of 32 million acres (13 million ha) per year.

The Lungs of Our Planet

By cutting down our forests, we are not only robbing many plant and animal species of their habitat, but we are also hurting ourselves. We are reducing our planet's ability to absorb carbon dioxide from the atmosphere, or air. This is making the problem of climate change worse. When trees disappear, there is nothing to hold down soil, and wind and water blow and wash it away.

The United Nations, the World Bank, and many nations are working to stop deforestation, however. Countries such as Bolivia have set up programs to pay farmers not to cut down their trees. They are instead encouraged to farm in ways that work with the forest. These include setting up beehives and harvesting honey. Canada and the United States set aside areas that are protected from **logging**, and require forestry companies to plant new trees to replace the ones they cut down. This helps protect the soil in areas where trees are cut down so the forest can grow again.

If the current rate of cutting down rain forests continues, it is possible there may be no rain forests left in 100 years.

Eco Up Close

The northern spotted owl lives in the old growth forests of Oregon, Washington, and Idaho. It hunts wood rats and other small animals at night. The owl has difficulty adapting to logged areas, or forests with younger trees that have less space for the owls to build their nests. In the early 1990s, environmentalists demanded that logging must be stopped in old growth forests to protect the spotted owl. Loggers and environmentalists argued over whether the threat to the owl was more important than the loss of jobs that would result if logging was stopped.

**northern
spotted owl**

Saving Forests

Many forests of the world have been cut down, destroying the habitat of many animals such as the parrots below. However, some people are working to protect what is left and to allow the old forests to regrow. This will take a lot of hard work. Here are some ways you can help to save forests, too.

What You Can Do

Write to your politicians and tell them to protect forests from development.

Use less paper. Make sure you use recycled paper. Recycle what you do use after you are done with it.

Plant trees. Some cities offer free seedlings that you can plant in your backyard. You can also join groups such as GROW (www.growforests.org) that can tell you more about tree-planting activities near where you live.

Activity:

Catching and Holding Water

Find out how the bromeliad plant catches and holds water and dirt, and how this creates a healthy soil in which other plants can grow.

You Will Need:

- Healthy pineapple with green leaves
- Sharp knife
- Spoon
- Potting soil
- Clay or plastic flower pot to hold the pineapple
- Adult supervision

Instructions

1. Have an adult cut the top off the pineapple, leaving roughly 3 inches (8 cm) of the fruit along with the leaves. Save the rest of the pineapple to eat later.
2. Place the pineapple top in the flower pot and leave it to dry for about 24 hours.
3. Cut away the outside of the pineapple, leaving the core of the fruit and the leaves.
4. Fill the flower pot with potting soil, until it is about 3 inches (8 cm) deep. Put the pineapple in the soil. Make sure the soil covers the core, and the leaves are in the air.
5. Put the flower pot with the pineapple in a sunny place. Water it whenever the soil gets dry.
6. When the pineapple grows new green leaves, you can put the plant outside in warm weather.
7. Observe what happens, especially after it rains. Does water pool in the leaves? Does dirt gather? Can you spot insects and worms?

step 1

step 3

step 4

The Challenge

Present your experiment to others with the following questions:

- What is it about the pineapple's leaves that help them gather water and dirt?
- What does the plant provide to the insects and other animals that you found on it?
- Is the pineapple a mini-ecosystem?

Glossary

Please note: Some bold-faced words are defined in the text

abiotic factors Nonliving parts of an ecosystem, such as water and soil

adapt Change over long periods of time or many generations

advantage A better ability

algae A group of organisms that have chlorophyll and can make their own food, but are not plants

amphibians Animals such as frogs and salamanders that begin life in water, then live on land as adults

apex predator An animal at the top of the food chain, which have few, if any, predators of their own

bacteria Living organisms made up of only one cell

biodiversity The variety of plant and animal life in an ecosystem or other area on Earth

biotic factors Living parts of an ecosystem, such as plants and animals

burrowing Digging holes or tunnels under the ground

carbon dioxide A gas produced when living things breathe out

chlorophyll A green substance in plants that changes sunlight and carbon dioxide into energy, which is stored as sugar and used by the plant for food

climate change A process in which the environment changes to become warmer, colder, drier, or wetter than normal. This can occur naturally, or it can be caused by human activity

coniferous Describing an evergreen tree that produces cones and has needles or scale-like leaves

deciduous Describing a type of tree with leaves that grow in the spring and the summer, and are dropped in the fall

dominate To have the most of

dormant When an organism goes into a long period of inactivity to survive

ecology The branch of biology that deals with organisms and their relationships to one another and to their physical surroundings

endangered At risk of dying out

equator The imaginary line along Earth that is the same distance from the north pole and the south pole

erosion The process in which rock or soil is worn or washed away by water, wind, and ice

estuaries Bodies of water where rivers meet the ocean and where fresh water and salt water mix

evergreen Trees that have leaves that do not dry out and fall off as a result of the changes of the season

fertile Having, or capable of producing, an abundance of vegetation

food chain A chain of organisms in which each member uses the member below as food

food web The interlinked food chains in an ecosystem

fungi Organisms, such as mold, that absorb food from their environment

habitat The natural environment of an animal or plant

hibernate When an animal reduces its activity and sleeps for weeks or months at a time to save its energy

interrelationships The relationships between many different organisms and their environment

keystone species A species that plays such an important role in its environment, that it affects many other organisms

logging Cutting down trees to use the wood to make goods such as paper or furniture

mammal A warm-blooded animal that has lungs, a backbone, and hair or fur, and drinks milk from its mother's body

migrate To travel to another area for food or to reproduce

monoculture An area with a large number of organisms all of the same species

nesting chamber A place an animal builds a nest in which to lay eggs and to raise young

nutrients Substances that allow organisms to thrive and grow

organisms Living things

overgrowth The area above the canopy in a forest

oxygen A gas found in air that living things need to live

photosynthesis The process in which plants use sunlight to change carbon dioxide and water into food and oxygen

predators Animals that hunt other animals for food

reptiles Animals, such as lizards and snakes, that have scales and that rely on the surrounding temperature to warm or cool their body

resistance The ability to prevent something from having an effect

salt marshes Shallow places on the ocean shore full of still salt water, where plants grow

savannas Areas of land in a warm climates where grasses are the main plant, often with scattered trees

species A group of animals or plants that are similar and can produce young

spore A small piece of an organism, usually a single cell, that grows into a new organism once it lands on ground that can let it grow

tidal flats Bodies of water fed by the movement of tides

tropical Describing a hot and humid climate

ultraviolet A type of radiation from sunlight that can cause sunburn and skin cancer

Learning More

Find out more about Earth's precious forest ecosystems.

Books

Godkin, Celia. *Fire! The Renewal of a Forest*. Markham, Ont.: Fitzhenry & Whiteside, 2008.

Greenaway, Theresa. *Jungle*. New York, NY: DK Publishing, 2009.

Tagliaferro, Linda. *Explore the Deciduous Forest*. Mankato, MN: Capstone, 2006.

Tagliaferro, Linda. *Explore the Tropical Rain Forest*. Mankato, MN: Capstone, 2007.

Waldron, Kathleen Cook, and Ann Walsh. *Forestry, A-Z*. Victoria, BC: Orca Book Publishers, 2008.

Websites

Find out more about different types of forests at:
http://wwf.panda.org/about_our_earth/about_forests/types

Visit the American Forests site to find out about protecting forests at:
www.americanforests.org

Find out more about taiga and temperate forest biomes:
http://kids.nceas.ucsb.edu/biomes/index.html

For a career in ecology, log on at:
http://kids.nceas.ucsb.edu/ecology/careers.html

Index